D1084201

WITHDRAWN

The World of Living Things

FOLLETT FAMILY LIFE EDUCATION PROGRAM

The World of Living Things

Esther K. Meeks and Elizabeth Bagwell

Follett Publishing Company   Chicago   New York

Photographic Credits

Cover picture by Robert Goodman, Black Star

Alpha Photo Associates, Inc., 7 left and upper right, 17 right; Bjorn Bolstad, Photo Researchers, Inc., 30 lower right; Allen Carr, 6 upper left, 8 upper left, 12 (all three), 14 (all nine), 15 (all three), 16 lower left and upper and lower right, 24 upper and lower left, 45 top; Chestnut House, 6 lower left; Alford W. Cooper, Photo Researchers, Inc., 23 upper right; Ben Dennison, 34 top; Freelance Photographers Guild, Inc., 2 lower left and upper right, 7 lower right, 8 lower right, 35 left and right; M. Grassi from Shostal, 23 lower right; Syd Greenberg, Photo Researchers, Inc., 10 top and bottom, 11 lower right; E. Hartmann, Magnum Photos, Inc., 44 right; Declan Haun, Black Star, 26 right, 28 top, 36 right, 37 upper and lower right, 38 upper and lower left, 41 (all five), 43, 45 lower left, 47 lower right; Wallace Kirkland, 8 lower left, 19; R. Leahy from Shostal, 25 top; Karl Maslowski, Photo Researchers, Inc., 16 upper left; Michael Mauney, Black Star, 2 upper left, 13 (both), 26 upper and lower left, 28 bottom, 30 upper and lower left, 36 left, 37 upper and lower left and middle right, 38 upper and lower right, 39 (all three), 40 (all five), 42 top and bottom, 44 left, 46 upper left and upper right, 47 upper and lower left and upper right; McCartney, Photo Researchers, Inc., 3; Dan McCoy, Black Star, 34 bottom; L. John McCue, Photo Researchers, Inc., 17 left; L. B. Nicholson, Jr., Photo Researchers, Inc., 24 right; Shostal, 2 lower right, 23 left, 45 lower right; Stanfield, Black Star, 6 right and middle left; Paul Thomas, Black Star, 7 middle right, 9 top; A. Upitis from Shostal, 25 bottom; Fred Ward, Black Star, 9 bottom

Illustrations by Tak Murakami

Designed by Chestnut House

Standard Book Number 695-89674-1   Trade Binding
Standard Book Number 695-49674-3   Library Binding
Standard Book Number 695-29674-4   Educational Binding

Library of Congress Catalog Card Number: 69-13380

Second Printing J

Consultants

John G. Chaltas
Associate Professor of Education
University of New Hampshire
formerly Director of Instruction
Glencoe, Illinois Public Schools

Tess Cogen
Family Life Educator
formerly Director, Family Life Education
The Association for Family Living

Willard Z. Kerman, M.D.
Pediatrician
Past Member and President
Glencoe, Illinois Board of Education

Curtis C. Melnick
Associate Superintendent
Chicago Public Schools

Edward Victor
Professor of Science Education
Northwestern University

Living things

Flower
fly

Daddy
longlegs

Mallard ducks

Rabbit

Deer

tle

Living things

Spiders are living things.
They can make new living
things like themselves.

Robins are living things.

They can make new living things like themselves.

Cats are living things.
They can make new living things like themselves.

12

People are living things.
They can make new living things like
themselves.

Bean plants are living things.

This bean plant can make new living things like itself.

A new plant can grow from each of the seeds.

DAVID MOHRHARDT FROM
NATIONAL AUDUBON SOCIETY

This maple tree can make new living things like itself.

A new tree can grow from each seed.

16

17

Cuckoo eggs

Meadowlark eggs

King snake and eggs

Turtle eggs

Living things can also come from eggs.

Some eggs are little.

Some eggs are big.

Each of them can be the start of a new living thing.

18

Frog with eggs

Some eggs are laid in
water.

These eggs need water
to grow in.

These eggs do not have
hard shells.

Canada geese

Birds lay eggs.

The eggs have hard shells.

The mother bird sits on the eggs to keep them warm.

When the babies are ready to be born, they peck their way out of the shells with their beaks.

20

Snake eggs

Most reptiles lay eggs.
Reptile eggs do not
have hard shells.

They feel more like
rubber.

Reptiles lay their
eggs on the ground or
in hollow logs.

The sun and air keep
the eggs warm until the
babies are ready to be
born.

Rabbit

Elephant

Bear

Some animals do not lay eggs, but their babies come from eggs that are inside the mother's body.

These eggs are very tiny.

They have no shells.

The babies grow inside the mother's body until they are ready to be born.

Each picture shows a baby that grew inside its mother's body.

23

Rose and daisy   Corn

When living things are grown up,
they can make new living things like
themselves.

24

Bull

Cow

Plants and animals have special parts that make seeds or eggs.

25

Your mother is a female.
If you are a girl, you
are a female, too.

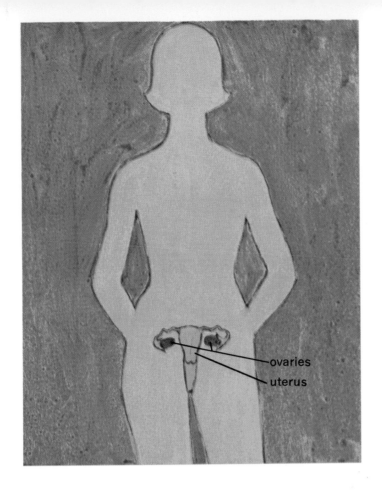

Females look different from males.

Eggs are in two special places in
a female body.

They are called the ovaries (OH-vuh-reez).

There is another special place in
a female body where the egg can grow
into a new baby.

This place is called the womb, or
uterus (YOO-ter-us).

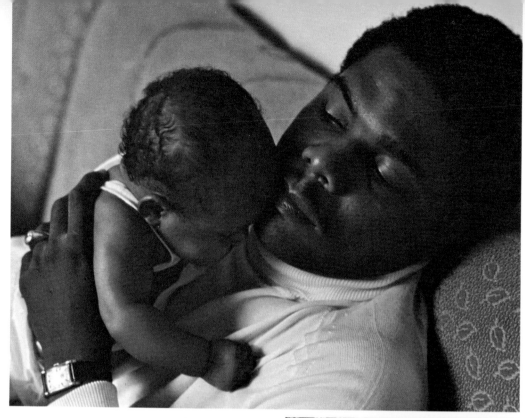

Your father is a male.
If you are a boy, you
are a male, too.

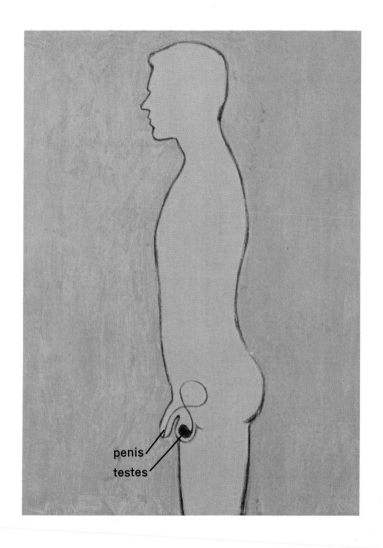

penis

testes

Special parts of your body show that you
are a male.

These parts are called the penis
(PEE-nus) and the testes (TESS-teez).

The testes of a grown-up male make
many, many tiny sperms.

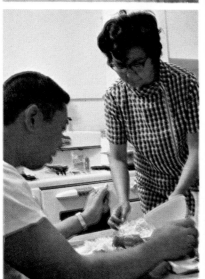

Ducks

Penguins

In people and in animals, the egg cannot make a new living thing by itself.

The egg needs something special from the father.

It needs a sperm.

30

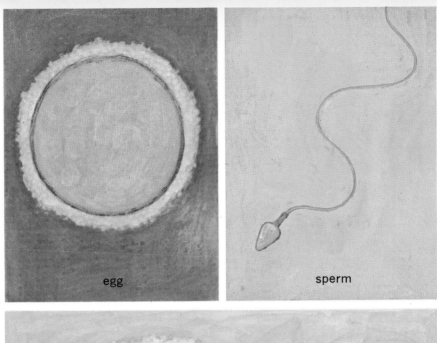

egg

sperm

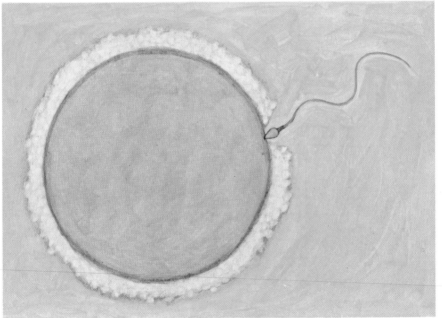

When the sperm from the male joins
with the egg from the female, a new
life begins.

At first it is very tiny.

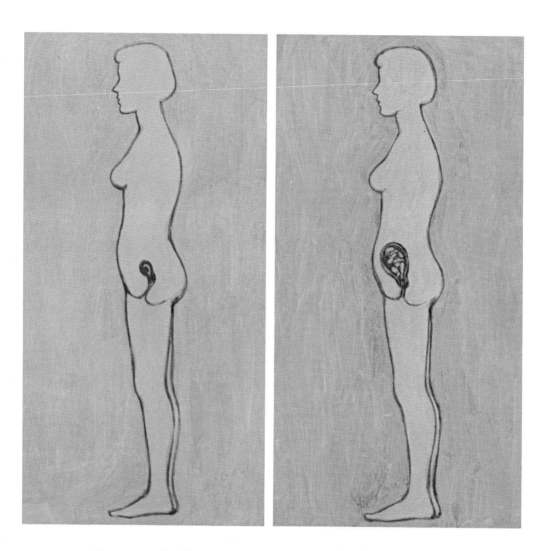

A human baby is very very tiny when
its life begins.

As days and weeks pass, it grows.

It begins to look like a baby.

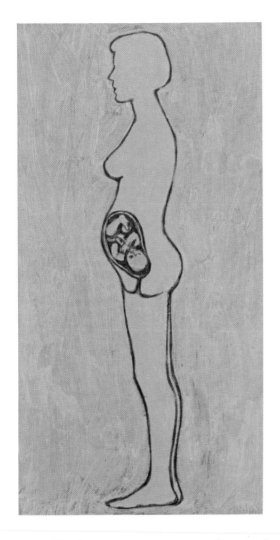

All the time it is safe and warm inside
its mother's body.

As the baby grows bigger, the mother
looks bigger.

The mother's uterus stretches to hold
the baby as it grows.

ADMITTING

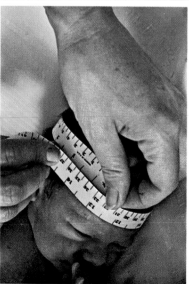

The father and mother are happy.

They are going to have a new baby to love and care for.

They get things ready that the baby will need.

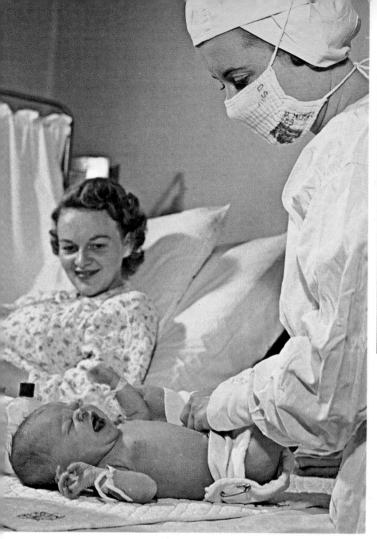

Most babies are born in hospitals.
Doctors and nurses take good care
of the mothers and babies.
In a few days, the father brings
the mother and the new baby home.

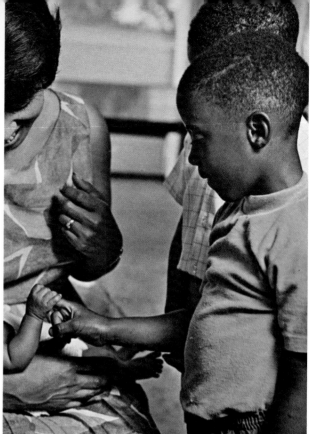

Human babies need a lot of love and care.

It seems that all a new baby can do is cry and sleep and eat.

Other people need to do everything for the baby.

Older brothers and sisters can help take care of the baby.

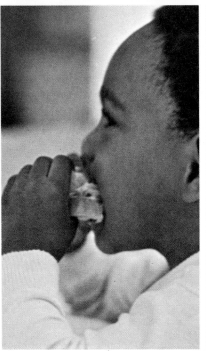

Parents care for their children because
they love them.

They see that they have food to eat.

They see that they have clothes to wear.
They see that their children get enough
sleep and keep clean.

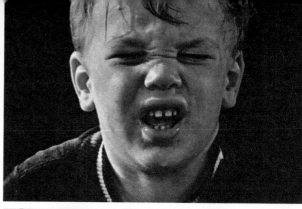

Parents do other things
for their children, too.

They teach them how to
live together in their own
family.

They teach them how to
live with other people.

Some families have
many children.
Some have just one
or two.
Some families have both
boys and girls.
Some have just boys.
Some have just girls.

Some families do not always have
both parents.

Then just the mother or the father takes
care of the children.

44

Grandmother and grandfather may help.
Older children can help, too.
All kinds of families love each other and
live and work together.

Fathers work.
Many mothers work, too.
They work to get money
for food and clothes and
homes for their families.

Being a family means living together.
It means sharing work and play.
It means sharing good times and bad
times, too.
Being a family means loving each other.
It means trying to make each other happy.